Then *&* **Now**
TRURO

The village of St Clement is shown during a flood, *c.* 1900. The house behind the trees is the vicarage and it was much later when the Revd O'Flynn was vicar there, that his wife suggested cutting a culvert through the vicarage garden to alleviate flooding. It worked and such bad flooding, as can be seen here, became a thing of the past. The water can be seen pouring down the road from the village to the creek and a boat was necessary to transport people where they would normally walk.

Then & Now
TRURO

COMPILED BY
CHRISTINE PARNELL

TEMPUS

Tempus Publishing Limited
The Mill, Brimscombe Port,
Stroud, Gloucestershire, GL5 2QG

ISBN 0 7524 2227 8

Typesetting and origination by
Tempus Publishing Limited
Printed in Great Britain by
Midway Colour Print, Wiltshire

Truro Secondary Modern school's football team of 1947 line up for the camera wearing their green and yellow strip. From left to right, back: Leon Penna, Billy Bray, Alf Polmear, Roy Stribley, Jackie Grose, Stanley Richards, Roy Sweet, Mr Trevor Broad. Front row: Stanley Holding, Dennis Barnicoat, Billy Kent, Brian Rapsey, Teddy Wearne.

CONTENTS

ACKNOWLEDGEMENTS

I would like to express my sincere thanks to all those who have lent me photographs, given me information and helped me to arrange all the modern pictures. They are: John and Pat Allam, Vera Blewett, Jacqui and Roy Bray, Harold Brown, Pat Carveth, John Colston, Brian Craven, John Crowther, Margaret Davis, Les Douch, Hazel Dunn, Beverley Dunstan, Joyce Gill, Pamela Glasson, Brian Head, Roger and Ros Heayn, Brian Hocking, J. Arnold Hodge, Jennifer Hosken, Ella Knight, John and Kay McBride, Andy McNally, Margaret Mitchell, Jacqui and Michael Nancarrow, Patricia O'Flynn, Maureen Pascoe, Mrs Pomeroy, Mike and Sheila Richardson, Audrey Settle, Dennis Smith, Roy Stribley, Paul and Simon Vage, Muriel and Ken Vigus, Mr Wilcocks, Doris Wilson and Edith Wilson.

Special thanks are due to my husband, Peter for all his help and photography and to my son David for his research and advice.

If I have overlooked anybody please accept my apologies.

An 1846 etching of Truro shows how small it was in comparison to the town today. Lemon Bridge is a recognisable landmark, as is the old St Mary's parish church and the hospital on the left. The Customs House stands guard over the river ready to collect any dues.

INTRODUCTION

Most people know that once a building has been demolished or remodelled, or a shop has changed hands or perhaps a new road has been built, within a very short time it is difficult to remember the way it used to be. This is especially the case in a town where shops are coming and going all the time, one-way traffic systems appear and new roads are built around the outskirts. This has happened with Truro as with many other towns in the country and some people hanker for the way that things were.

I hope that this collection of old photographs which has been matched as nearly as possible with the modern equivalent will remind people of the 'good old days'. Not that they were really so very good, most people were poorer, had less opportunity to make a good living and perhaps better themselves, and some of the things we take for granted today such as cars and holidays were luxuries for the wealthy. Although many of the old photographs evoke a feeling of a more leisurely pace of life, some things about the city now were very noticeable to me. Today we have flowers and trees all over the city and many times I found that the view I wanted was obscured by a tree, but the overall effect these days is a much greener, lighter town. It is no wonder we do so well in the Britain In Bloom contest!

Yet again people have been very generous with their photographs and I am sure I have captured a good mix of town, hobbies, people and the workplace. When we asked people for permission to take modern photographs, they were always helpful. I should like to mention James from Penrose Outdoors, who took us out onto the roof, the assistant manager of Somerfield's and Mr Pat Williams of SEC, who sent me an electrician in a hoist. Some of the modern photographs will already be out of date before the book is published as Truro is the focus of so much development at the moment. The Green, Lemon Quay and Fairmantle Street will be unrecognisable for a while but soon we will get used to the new arrangements and memories of the old will dim, that is until you open this book.

I am most grateful to all the people listed in the acknowledgements but also, as usual, to Jo Elsome-Jones who wrote pieces in the local newspapers telling people what I was doing and asking them to search their albums. They searched and when the dreadful wet winter weather cleared up my husband and I got busy with the camera. This is the result, I hope you like it.

Chistine Parnell
March 2001

A birds-eye view of the end of Boscawen Bridge around 1960, has changed so much since Morlaix Avenue was built that it is almost unrecognisable today. The No. 46 Newquay bus is probably on its way to the bus depot, built in 1947 and due for demolition in 2001 year. At the time this photograph was taken the large brick building was part of the premises of W. Penrose and Sons. They were sail makers and to the left of the main building they had an annex advertising boats and tents. Penroses had the distinction of making the largest tent in the world. The firm still exists and this photograph was taken from the roof of the building they now occupy.

This fascinating photograph of Truro was taken before the cathedral was finished in 1910 and with some of the 1904 viaduct in place, so it probably dates from 1905-1906. The Green is clearly a green space with Green House, the customs house, looking towards the river. Many interesting features are visible, Lemon Bridge, the smelting works chimneys in Malpas Road and of course Brunel's old wooden viaduct. The spires of St George's Methodist church and the spires of the Congregational church in River Street can be seen, as can the towers of St George's church and, on the skyline, Kenwyn church. The timber yards on the left are quite an eyesore but were an important part of Truro's industry and gave employment to many.

Chapter 1

THE TOWN

are loaded with parcels, the one for St Columb even has a bicycle on top. Burton's China Galleries later moved premises to King Street, opposite the cathedral and 'Burton' can still be seen in the brickwork of the new building. Today the post office is next to the old assembly rooms. Opened in 1789 or thereabouts, the elegant façade is decorated with Wedgwood plaques. The rooms ceased to be used for entertainment when in the late 1880s new assembly rooms by The Quay were in use. Over the years the building has been many things including a garage and an estate agent. Today it houses a baker's shop. The shoe shop in the corner is currently undergoing a facelift and the whole area looks particularly attractive in summer with many hanging baskets.

Taken in the early 1900s, we see High Cross, crowded with horse buses that came in regularly from the country. One covered the Summercourt and St Columb area and although all the buses

King Street around 1920 was just as much a shopping street as it is today. The tailor's shop belonged to John Osborne; Eastman's, the butcher was still there in the 1960s and changed in due course to Dewhurst and G.H. Philp, the photographer, is to be thanked for many of the old views of the town that still survive today. His postcards are now collectors' items. Although the shop fronts have changed, the buildings themselves are much the same. A building society and a travel agent have appeared and there are phone boxes on the corner, all things far removed from the picture eighty years ago. This part of King Street is very close to High Cross, believed to be the oldest part of Truro. Traders crossing from the Gannel to the Fal would come into Truro

over the Pydar Street area and the town is thought to have grown up around the cross which the Cornish historian, Charles Henderson suggested was older then Truro itself.

hundred of Pydar and leads out to Pydar from Truro, which is in the old hundred of Powder. In the 1960s photograph there was still a two-way traffic system but today the tank trap flower bed, bollards and seats denote a pedestrianised area, although it is not totally traffic free so one has to be watchful. Cupola on the right of the new photograph have steps built to their door and further down the road what was once two shops is now one, Dixons. A coat of paint makes Hawke's, the tailors, look more cheerful than it used to and the Halifax Building Society has removed the shop window used when it was the Calor Gas shop and replaced it with a window in the original style.

Pydar Street is one of the most ancient routes leading to the town and was referred to in 1464 as Strete Pydar. It takes its name from the

This side of Pydar Street is more noticeably different today than the other side of the road, which still retains much of its original character. In the picture taken in the 1930s the building of the armoury dominates. It was the headquarters of the Fourth and Fifth Battalion of the Duke of Cornwall's Light Infantry, part of the Territorial Army. Farther down we can see the sign of the London Inn and the front of the library. It was in this area that John Nicol Tom, a maltster, built his house. There are fantastic tales about his life after he left Truro and went insane. He proclaimed he was the Messiah and the owner of the Earl of Devonshire's estate, amongst other things. The

building on the left of the new picture was built in the 1960s for Tesco and later taken over by C & A. This photo was taken two weeks before C & A closed their doors for ever.

One of Truro's famous buildings was the unusually shaped post office in High Cross, much loved by the local people. It was built in 1886 and the architect was Silvanus Trevail who was responsible for many important buildings in the county. According to some who worked there it was an inconvenient building with many corridors and small rooms but nevertheless it was a sad day in June 1974 when it was demolished. The old Unicorn Inn had been knocked down to make way for the post office, as had The Brick House, a building owned by the borough. It was unusual for Truro, where brick is not a common building material. It was sometimes known as 'The House by the Cross'. It is interesting to see the sign attached to the lamp-post on the right of the picture. It says, 'Keep to your right'; did people coming down King Street have to keep to their right as well? The Marks and Spencer building now occupies the corner site.

Recognisable as Boscawen Street, these photographs are similar, yet worlds apart in the everyday lives of Truronians. The taxis for hire stand in the middle of the street around 1900, and a handcart is parked neatly at the kerb outside the Red Lion. Behind the horse trough is a shop selling cookers and gas fires and next door are dining rooms. The shop on the ground floor of London House appears to have rolls of carpet or linoleum in the window. On the right-hand side of St Nicholas Street we can just get a glimpse of Criddle and Smith's. James Jenkin Smith came to Truro from Bristol in 1870 and later went into partnership with W.J. Criddle, who was an ironmonger, cabinet maker and upholsterer in King Street. The shop in

St Nicholas Street was sold to Dingle's of Plymouth in 1966. Today the Nationwide Building Society occupies the site of the dining rooms, Boggia has the shop that sold the gas fires and Tony Pryce's sports shop, is in London House.

quite a time delay for an exposure taken at lighting-up time and consequently many of the figures are shadowy but nevertheless it makes a nice picture. The lamplighter is actually on top of the ladder, lighting a gas lamp and two lamps are lit in the office on the right. On the wall of the municipal building is a poster advertising The Foot Guards, who were presumably coming to Truro. The modern photograph was not able to be taken in the dark, as during the Christmas period the decorations would have obscured the view and by the time they had been taken down and the rain had stopped for a while, the evenings were lighter. The pump and the fountain are gone and the war memorial is now in a prominent position outside Woolworth's.

Although the date of the old photograph is not known, it must have been taken in the early 1900s, judging by the clothes on sale in the window of Gill's. Presumably there was

Truro is very proud of its war memorial which was unveiled on 15 October 1922 by the Lord Lieutenant of Cornwall, Mr J.C. Williams of Caerhayes. Possibly this photograph shows the first Remembrance Day since the unveiling, with enough floral tributes to cover half the memorial. Heard & Sons organ factory, N. Gill & Sons ladies' tailors and Jordans printing works are in the background. Obtaining a modern photograph proved difficult because of the traffic. The taxi rank is on the area where the fountain used to stand and the 3 Zero café, with its large 1960s-style windows, has replaced Jordans.

London House is on the corner of Lower Lemon Street with Boscawen Street and used to have a W.H. Smith shop on two floors with a library and reading room upstairs. Books could be borrowed at a charge of threepence (3d) each. The shop window extended round the corner into Lemon Street. The earlier photograph is from the 1960s and was taken just as the modernization was beginning. The name 'London House' and all the windows on both sides were covered over with the small white tiles that are still there today. Smith's is now in Pydar Street and for many years a sports shop has been in London House. The Co-operative Building Society has gone and Boggia has moved across from the other side of Boscawen Street. About fifty years ago there was a baker's called Millican's in this area and an opening to Back Quay, which has long since been closed off.

Henry Hodge pulls his handcart through Lower Lemon Street, possibly in 1910, when the town was decorated for the coronation of King George V. Henry worked for a brewery in Victoria Square. There are two cyclists in the street and a postman on foot with a large sack of letters. A pony and trap is waiting at the end of the road. The old fire badge can be seen on the Royal Hotel so if the hotel had caught fire back in the days when insurance was paid to individual companies, they would have had their fire extinguished providing the right company attended. If the wrong company had driven past, presumably they would have ignored the fire! Dating from 1800 the Royal was formerly known as Pearce's Hotel and in 1859 was a stopping point for the Quicksilver coach which left Falmouth each morning bound for London. In the modern photograph, cars fill the street and a traffic island stands where people could once lean on the bridge and look at the river.

considerably but they are always well tended by the City Council. The old granite setts unfortunately have been removed and modern material is used as a road surface. The building on the left is The Royal Hotel which was so named when Prince Albert visited it. Queen Victoria had had a busy schedule and remained on board her yacht, leaving Albert to visit alone. Today the stonework has been cleaned, removing all the soot and the royal coat of arms over the door is brightly painted.

Although the buildings in Lower Lemon Street thankfully have not changed, there are many subtle differences in these two pictures taken some forty-five years apart. The most noticeable change is that The Red Lion has gone. Built as the town house of the Foote family in 1671, it had been an inn since 1769 but was so badly damaged by a runaway lorry in 1967 that it had to be demolished. The Co-op grocery shop that takes its place cannot be compared favourably to the beautiful old building. The gas lamp has gone, we never see a policeman directing the traffic at the junction with Boscawen Street and the traffic is now one-way. The tank-trap style flower beds that have sprung up all over the town, narrow the street

This old postcard of 1897 is entitled 'Victoria Place' but although the photographer was standing in Victoria Place it is actually a view looking up St Nicholas Street to Boscawen Street. Amos Jennings's grocery store is on the left, it was later W.H. Smith after that store moved from London House and is now Foster's clothing store. Edwin Broad's department store is on the right with Radmore's dining rooms opposite. Interestingly the postcard was sent to a little girl in the south ward of the infirmary, by her mother. In today's picture the traffic system allows for an island on the junction to enable people to cross over safely. Radmore's is now Barratt's shoe shop and Edwin Broad's is a mobile phone shop. It was in St

Nicholas Street in 1958 that workmen digging up the road found the cross identified by Mr Douch, then curator of the museum, as the original cross which has now been replaced and is in its correct position in High Cross.

Although the older picture, taken around 1905, is entitled 'St Nicholas Street and Square', the square in which the photographer stood is known as Victoria Square even though the correct name is Victoria Place. The horse buses are parked where today the cars jostle for a twenty-minute parking space. The 'iron duke' gentlemen's toilet on the left of the old picture was removed many years ago, probably in the 1950s. Next door but one to the Victoria Hotel is Mallett's ironmongers shop, still thriving today but now in premises actually in Victoria Place. This area of town was the site of the West Bridge (the old bridge in Old Bridge Street formerly being known as the East Bridge). Foster's, behind the signpost in the new picture, is on the site of the old town mill.

When looking at Boscawen Street it is easy to imagine how it would have looked in the past. Middle Row was built in the mid-1300s and we know that in the eighteenth century the two roads formed by this row of buildings were called Market Street and Fore Street. This row contained the old Market House, which would have been opposite what we think of as the Midland Bank, now HSBC. It was in 1806 that Middle Row was pulled down and the Daniell Tablet was moved, later to be erected in the entrance to the City Hall. Dated 1615, it is inscribed, 'Who seks to find eternal tresure must use no guile in waight or measure' and is attributed to 'Ienken Daniell, Maior'. The Market House was on pillars and the council met in the rooms above, just as today the council chamber is in the

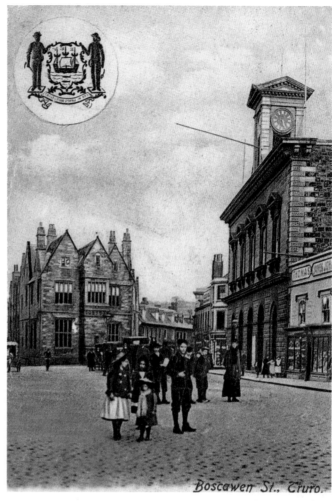

Boscawen St., Truro.

same building as the tablet. One of the buildings lost when Middle Row was demolished was the prison. Until 1921 the City Police station was housed in the municipal buildings, together with the courtroom, hence the saying, 'I'll have you under the clock' which was used to threaten those who misbehaved! At the end of Middle Row was the coinage hall. It was outside this building that John Wesley first preached to the people of Truro in 1776. The building on that site today houses tearooms and a pizza express.

As we can glimpse part of the war memorial in the old photograph, we know that it was taken sometime after 1922. On the left is Treleavens Café, advertising luncheons and teas and also, just beside the door, peach melba. Over thirty years later it was still a favourite place to go for a treat, or in my case, as a reward for behaving at the dentist! There are other tearooms advertised on the building behind the war memorial. Perhaps Truronians enjoyed eating out if they could afford it. Mr Vage's jeweller's shop is on the right. In the modern view the area looks much more cheerful. Mr Paul Vage and his son Simon have a larger shop with frilled blinds and hanging baskets. The pavement has been extended and a tree makes the area into an attractive square.

We are in Quay Street in this old photograph, taken in the 1920s, with Treleavens Café on the left. Treleavens was also a bakery and the company had a department which catered for various functions in the town. The building was demolished in the 1960s and later replaced with a modern structure. John Langdon's cycle shop is in St Mary's Street but today an electronics shop is in the same premises. Although Treleavens has gone, the building opposite on the right of the modern view is Blewett's the bakers and has been so for many years. There are mews shops beside Blewett's and also in the alleyway beside Langdon's old shop leading to the river. The blackboard advertising the Crab and Alehouse pub is referring to what many Truronians think of as The White Hart. Until its name was recently changed it had the distinction of being the pub which had retained its name the longest.

There have been many changes in the Trafalgar area of Truro over recent years. The old police station was knocked down but not until a new station had been built behind it and was fully operational. The new one was opened by Princess Anne in 1974 and actually won an award despite being built back to front. The Trafalgar Garage was opposite the police station and sold Commer and Sunbeam vehicles and Shell petrol. They also had a showroom next to the police station. St Austell Street was a narrow road lined with cottages. This has all changed and a much wider St Austell Street (because of the demolition of both the garage and the Lord Nelson) comes out into a large roundabout with traffic lights for use at busy times. The roundabout is well-planted with trees and shrubs and is especially attractive at Christmas when an illuminated display is placed there.

In the 1950s the area between Boscawen Bridge and Trafalgar Square had many little shops and was quite a thriving community. There was even a sub-post office which was run by Mr Luck. In 1953 Mary Waters (in the white coat), Doreen Trebilcock and another lady, stand outside Boscawen Dairy for a photograph. Mr and Mrs Trebilcock ran the shop and lived in the flat above. Lyons tea is advertised, as is Cadbury's, over the door. This was a long time before there was any ban on cigarette advertising, and both Turf and Players were offered for sale. As the year was 1953 one suspects that the large striped bows in the window were red, white and blue. Could this have been

Coronation Day? The site where the shop stood is currently the edge of a dual-carriageway and the only small shop in the area is the post office and store at Trafalgar.

Part of the changes in the Trafalgar area includes the top of Malpas Road. The Admiral Boscawen was knocked down in 1966, opening up a view of some of the cottages leading to Boscawen Bridge. Many of the cottages contained shops such as C.C. Clemens, seen here, and farther along the same road was a very good and well-used fish and chip shop. The road today is wider and leads to the Trafalgar roundabout with the Roman Catholic Church of 'Our Lady of the Portal and St Piran' across the way, built in 1972. The old Roman Catholic Church was in Chapel Hill. The large tree hides a garage on the site of the old Truro smelting works. Only one of their buildings survives and is still in use today as part of the garage.

The Britannia Inn was once owned by the borough but was sold in order to build a swimming pool for the town at Hendra. Unfortunately, in the local government reorganization in 1974, the pool passed from the City Council into the hands of Carrick District Council and as the years went on and the pool became older, it was necessary to close it and build a new one at Truro College. The Britannia Inn, however, still exists and is undergoing refurbishment. It now has a dual carriageway running alongside it, and the coach and car park, where once there was a bowling green, has been swept away and building works are in progress for a new coach park. The cars in the mid-1960s photograph are a Ford

Zephyr, a Wolseley and a Vauxhall Cresta. Two old Bedford country buses are parked nearby. The white one says 'Tregony' on its destination panel and perhaps it was a Lidgey's bus.

Britannia Inn. The impressive backs of Princes House, built for William Lemon in 1740 and The Mansion House, built for Thomas Daniell in 1760 are behind the clutter of shed-like buildings, some of which had been demolished by the time the modern photograph was taken. This was to make way for the Royal Bank of Scotland. The coaches and cars have had to move, as the area is now a building site. Much redevelopment is currently taking place, not only on The Green but also on Lemon Quay and although it does not make a very attractive picture it temporarily opens up views and will remind us in the future what the area looked like without the new development.

The Green seen in the 1970s was used as a coach and car park. It got its name from the bowling green which was situated at the rear of the

The Municipal Building in Boscawen Street was designed by the architect Christopher Eales and built in 1846-1847. Seen here in 1904 we also have a good view of the pump, the fountain and the horse trough. They have all since been moved. In November 1914 a fire broke out in the Municipal Buildings and the clock tower crashed down into the council chamber below. An anonymous donor paid for a replacement and an identical structure was built but the new clock face is white rather than the original black. The horse-drawn taxis parked in the street are facing the wrong way for the traffic system of today.

Edward Pellew, Lord Exmouth, who was involved in the abolition of slavery and Goldsworthy Gurney, who, because of his steam carriages, made standardized time throughout the country a necessity. On the back wall of the small building the arms of the city were beautifully painted and are a focus of school trips to the town. The Royal British Legion club was built on the vacant plot in the 1980s.

In 1259 Bishop Bronscombe came down from Exeter and consecrated the chapel of St Mary, which later became the parish church. When the church was pulled down, the south aisle was incorporated into the cathedral and narrow St Mary's Street runs alongside it. The Walpamur van is parked outside what was, in the 1960s, the Walpamur shop, selling decorating materials. The building used by this company was part of the old grammar school, founded in 1549 by Walter Borlase. Many pupils, who later became famous, studied there. They include Richard Lander, who discovered the source of the River Niger, Humphry Davy, famous for inventing the miners' safety lamp and discovering 'laughing gas' and Henry Martyn, a missionary who translated the Bible into many languages. Samuel Foote, the actor, studied there as did

Over the years many trees have grown in Truro, making it almost impossible to find the exact spot from which to take a photograph to match an earlier view. In this case the car rental building is just visible and the Design Bureau has long since been completed but the old St Andrew's chapel is missing. The Moorfield multi-storey car park takes up much of the space where the fair used to be set up when it came to town. Calenick Street has also changed in character over the years. Once it was a very rough area and the doss house was situated there although an elderly resident has said that it was perfectly safe for children to walk through the streets. His mother used to cook a Christmas dinner every year for one of the inmates and it was entrusted to a child to deliver it. Each year both the child and the dinner arrived safely!

The 1960s view of The Leats was taken during the time when it was forbidden to do anything other than walk through this narrow road. The park keeper patrolled The Leats area and this part was the farthest section from the park. Even bicycles were pushed and not ridden. On the left, the channel of the leat can be seen with granite slabs crossing it at intervals to give access to the houses there. The first crossing led to the big house owned by musicians Mr and Mrs Lightbown. Farther down there was access to The Peoples' Palace, an old-time leisure centre which catered for games such as snooker, skittles, boxing and more genteel pastimes such as a choir. The old Ebenezer chapel became Cornish's sale rooms and was later knocked down. Today Elizabeth House, the Job Centre, stands on the site and the leat is covered over. Cars and lorries rumble up and down and Mr Lightbown's house is the office of The Transport and General Workers' Union.

Many properties that were family homes in Truro in the past are business properties today. This is particularly true of the houses in Edward Street and Castle Street, many of them being solicitors' offices close to the court. This 1935 or 1936 photograph was taken in Old Bridge Street. The house is No. 10, the home of the Nicholls family and the children are outside on the narrow pavement. They are Frances, Pamela, Frank, Pauline and Barbara. Their cousin Jean is the small girl in the gymslip. Today this house is Walker's Fish and Chip Shop and Restaurant. The pavement is just as narrow and of course the road is festooned with yellow lines. The shoppers' short-stay car park is just across the road and a very handy place to park long enough to get a meal.

granddaughter Tamsin made regular trips to the 'donkey field' as it was known. The field is between Treyew Road and Crescent Rise and was home to a family of well-loved and cared for donkeys including Bunty, Corrie and Angus. People from all over Truro used to visit them and for two elderly ladies from the nearby residential home it was a pleasure to forego their cracker biscuits and save them for the donkeys. Before long the county council needed to extend and the donkeys' owner had to move the animals and take down their stable to make room for the offices and car park which is on the site today. The fence on the right of the new picture is the same one that the donkeys are standing beside.

The 1989 photograph, although hardly 'archive', shows that many changes have taken place in a short space of time. Byryn Mitchell with daughter Christine Parnell and

John Cooper Furniss had a bakery in King Street around 1877 which did so well that he moved to Church Lane, known as Cathedral Lane today. This probably benefited his business even more as the workmen from the cathedral would have been right on his doorstep and, no doubt, often hungry. His cakes, gingerbreads and fairings were renowned and as well as his shop he supplied the refreshment room at the railway station – wheeling his handcart all the way up Richmond Hill at regular intervals. Almost a hundred years later in the factory in St Austell Street, Valerie Osborne, Roy

Chapter 2
WORK AND
EDUCATION

Lean and Bill Thomas inspect the merchandise while out in the town everyone knew what was cooking by the delicious aroma wafting around!

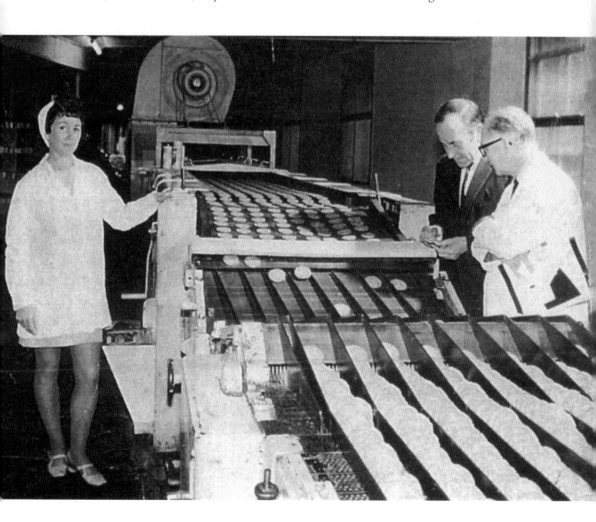

Street. The staff in 1943 are, from left to right, back row: Frank Martin (manager), Hogarth Turner, Bonzo Bird, Len Tilbrook, ? Page, John Corin, Raymond Brown, Lloyd White, Gaffer Tremayne, Clifford Hosken, Trevor Higgins, Powell Hollow, Billy Blight. Front row: Ruth Pearce (Gummow), Miss May, Nellie Pascoe, Gwen Harris, Barbara Spray. Today the staff have a corporate uniform which has various combinations of blouse, skirt and trousers. The bank is painted in a light colour and notices adorn the walls. The use of computers almost certainly means having less staff but four Cornish girls took a few moments out to pose. Jo Hocking is sitting at her computer with Lynn Johns beside her. The two ladies standing are Heather Lake (left) and Melanie Sweet.

Banks have changed with the times and instead of being sombre places which over-awed many people, are now much brighter and more accessible. Barclay's Bank is situated on the corner of St Nicholas Street and King Street and there is another branch in Lemon

Lennards' shoe shop also had a shoe repair factory. Shoes from all over Cornwall and Devon were brought here to be repaired and there was also a contract with English China Clay. The shoes to be repaired had to be collected from the railway station arrived in large wicker baskets and they had to be ready to be sent back by 4.30 p.m. The staff of the repair department, around 1957 are: Jack and Doris Nancarrow, -?-, Derek Boughton, E. Cocks, Bert Lamerton, Tom Matthews, Trevor Cowell and Nick Carter. The story told of Derek Boughton is that one day he had fallen off a roof and, thinking he deserved some time off work, he started the day limping on one leg. Later he forgot which leg he had hurt and limped on the other. He ended the day limping on both

legs! In due course, Mr Carter became manager of the shop. Peter Mallett, on the left, and Ricky Kempthorne, repair the shoes of Truronians today at the Creation Centre.

was rationed he was responsible for loading the correct amount of lamb onto the lorry for RNAS Culdrose at Helston. Seen here during the big freeze of 1947 he is actually working in a temperature of 22 degrees below freezing but he still wonders today if it was colder outside the storeroom! The closest shop to this depot where one can buy meat today is the Somerfield supermarket in Victoria Place. Until recently they had a butcher working behind the scenes preparing the meat for sale but these days all the meat comes to the store pre-packaged. Richard Manuel, who worked on the delicatessen counter is seen showing some lamb and beef.

J. Arnold Hodge is known to many people in Truro as a retired master butcher who kept a shop in Frances Street for many years. He was a pork butcher whose famous pork sausages are still remembered. As a public-spirited person he was a long-standing member of Truro city council and at different times a member of Carrick district council and a county councillor. Retired now, he is a past mayor of Truro, a Freeman of the City of Truro and a Freeman of the City of London. In 1947, however, it was a different story. He was the store man at the Ministry of Food depot in City Road and as food

The Central Despatch department at the new county hall is a hive of activity but the staff managed to slow down for a couple of photographs. All incoming post is sorted and delivered to the correct department in the morning. Later in the day all the outgoing mail is also collected and taken back to Central Despatch for processing. As the site is spread out, the crates of mail for some offices are loaded into one of the little white vans and delivered in style. In the mid to late 1970s the staff included, from left to right: Byryn Mitchell, Don Johnson, Graham Pye and Eddie Pye. The lady and the man at the back had possibly come down with their post from another department. The modern

photograph shows Graham Pye, Colin Jennings, Tony Wyatt and Pete Stoddern.

Commander in Chief of the South East Command was the inspecting officer. However, as the Durham Light Infantry were approximately forty men below strength, John was in the group chosen to join them for another six weeks advanced training. This was at the time of the Suez crisis. Sapper Phillip McBride wanted to join the services so he started by joining the Truro Sea Cadets when he was aged eleven. When he was old enough he joined the corps of Royal Engineers and did his training at Bassingbourn in Hertfordshire. He is now pursuing his career with the Royal Signals. In the photograph Phillip, aged nineteen years, is holding the trophy he won as best recruit in August 2000. Before joining the army he was the mayor's cadet for twelve months and attended many civic functions and parades.

Before National Service was abolished all the local boys wondered where they would have to serve and which regiment they would join. John Colston (centre) and his comrades Billy Penfold (left) and Stuart Davey were destined for the Duke of Cornwall's Light Infantry. After ten weeks training at Bodmin barracks they passed out on 19 October 1956 and General Sir George Erskine, the

The arches of the 1904 viaduct form a backdrop to many of the old fire brigade photographs. In this one even the old toilet block in the park is in view. One of the more mundane jobs that had to be done was to keep all the vehicles clean and in tip-top condition. Here, around 1960, Ted Blake is leaning on the Austin van which looks as if it has had a good polish. The spotlight and the bell on the front were additions not found on private cars. Today the vans are Vauxhalls and are to be found lined up at fire brigade headquarters at Old County Hall. Martin Cleverly is standing beside a van in the modern version of the everyday working uniform. No cap and dungarees for him but a comfortable sweat shirt embroidered with the fire brigade logo. It is a far cry from the days of the

Truro City Volunteer Fire Brigade, founded in March 1868. There were thirty men under the command of Captain James Henderson. The fire station was in St Mary's Street where they had two fire engines and an escape. However firemen, who were elected by ballot, had to provide their own boots, axe and belt.

When the 1960 photograph was taken the fire brigade was based in St George's Road at Hendra as it had been since 1944. This was very useful for Jack Parnell, who lived just across the road. When he was younger he was usually the first to report for duty if an emergency occurred at night, as he would jump out of bed straight into his clothes which were laid out ready, into his boots, out of the door and across the road. Seen here, approaching retirement, he is on duty in the control room with Chris Helps (on the left) with the map and notice board behind them. The control room today is in the Old County Hall and is fully equipped with computers and the latest technology. Pointing at the map is Helen Knight with Stephanie Lovering standing by. Seated at his computer is Steve Lusty-Hoye.

Many of the men who joined Cornwall County Fire Brigade at its inception in 1948 were already firefighters who had been in the Auxiliary Fire Service and had served during the war years. One youngster who was asked at school what his father was doing to help the war effort, said that his father was fire-fighting in Turkey, having misunderstood the word 'Torquay'. Cyril Anstiss is working with the pump escape in Rotten Woods in the late 1950s, the appliance being the same red monster shown on p. 96. He is wearing a collar and tie with trousers, jacket and the inevitable cap whereas Martin Cleverly is wearing the modern gear with boots and special headgear with visor. The *City of Truro* had just returned from a mission to St Agnes and been made ready for any further

call-out. Fifty years ago St Agnes was a regular place for visits from the fire brigade, not on emergency calls but because the stores were kept there on the Cameron Estate. The officer in charge of stores would collate all the requests that came in from round the county and pack everything up, labelled for the correct fire station. He then worked out his route and delivered everything.

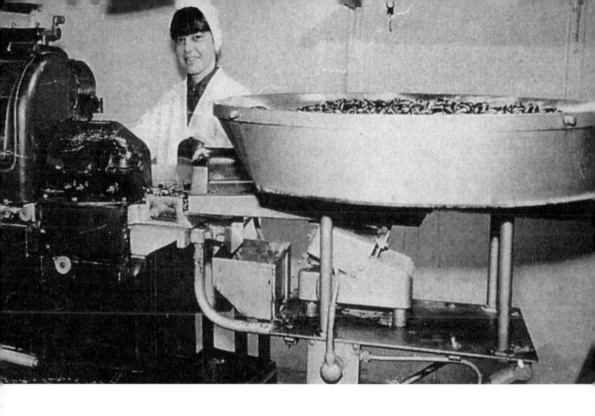

machinery. The tub appears to be full of boiled sweets, because as well as biscuits they also made sweets and peppermint rock. When John Cooper Furniss realised what a demand there was for his cakes and biscuits he formed a company with T. Chirgwin and W. Bennett in 1886 and started manufacturing at a larger scale than before on Duchy Wharf. He died in 1888 and left one hundred shares in the company to Truro city council in order that the income from them could be spent on coal for those in need, a charity which still exists today. John Colston is seen operating an entirely different type of machinery. As a saw doctor he is sharpening saws. He is wearing protective eyewear and boots with steel toecaps whereas a hat and white overalls was all that was necessary for Sandra Kent.

Sandra Kent is seen in the Furniss biscuit factory around 1960 using some very complicated-looking

Truro once had a castle situated on high ground between the Rivers Kenwyn and Allen. It was held by Richard de Lucy, the king's Chief Justiciar, although the castle probably existed long before he came to Cornwall in 1140. The town grew up in the shadow of his castle with the benefit to both the town's people and de Lucy derived from the charter procured by him. By 1270 the site of the castle was described as a 'placea', a vacant plot. It was once the area where the scavengers lived and the bull used for bull-baiting at High Cross was kept there. By 1840 the area was being cleared to build a cattle market. Market day was Wednesday, a contrast to Thursday, which was early closing. To accommodate the market there was a

railway halt there for the loading and unloading of cattle. Today we have the Crown Court on the site of the cattle market or, more appropriately, on the site of the old castle.

Work started on covering over the River Kenwyn between Lemon Quay and Back Quay in 1926 but until that time boats used to come right up the river to unload. The old photograph shows a Peerless lorry, driven by Mr Henry May, known as 'Yank', who worked for Western Counties Agriculture. The boat was carrying grain, which was loaded into the lorry. The new picture shows Lemon Quay car park complete with its selection of recycling bottle banks. The back of the Municipal Building is looking very smart, as it is now the main entrance to The Hall for Cornwall. Beside it is the 1930s style rear entrance to Woolworth's. The new fly-tower of The Hall for Cornwall completely blocks the view of the town clock except for the weather vane.

Many people fondly remember Fairmantle Street School. It came into being from an Anglican school of St John's church. First known as The Central School, it started in Tippet's Backlet but after ten years (around 1823) moved to a plot behind a house in Lemon Street. Fairmantle Street did not exist at that time. For a while it was a training school for teachers and in 1940 it was requisitioned by the government to house a volunteer force from the Channel Islands. When it was returned to the church and repairs had been carried out, it again opened as a school in 1949. By the early 1970s the pupils were being taught in the parish hall owing to the unsafe state of the

building. It is now gone and Mr Percy Beswetherick, the funeral director, has his offices and car park on the site.

The Education Act of 1870 stated that there must be a place in school for every child and that compulsory attendance at a school would shortly be introduced. At this time, like many other towns, Truro had a mixture of different types of schools. There were church schools situated close to their parent churches, non-conformist schools, known as British Schools, Dames Schools and even a Ragged School in Campfield Hill. In the changes that ensued, St Mary's Church School moved to larger premises in Pydar Street in 1891. This school continued in use until the 1960s. The building on the site now is Pydar House, home to the Ministry of Agriculture, Fisheries and Food, who had previously used the old teachers' training college in Agar Road.

Truro County Grammar School for Girls stood, from 1925 to 1993, on the site in Treyew Road which is now a Sainsbury's supermarket. The foundation stone was laid by The Right Honourable, the Lord Eustace Percy, MP, president of His Majesty's Board of Education. Tennis courts were to the side of the building and a hockey pitch behind, although in time some portable classrooms arrived to take up some of the open space. Stories say that the workmen whose job it was to demolish the building were almost in tears at tearing down such a well-built school. For the last few years of its life it was used as a sixth-form college, then it had to make way for the supermarket and the new college was built at Gloweth. Sainsbury's have used much of the original granite in their own building, which is in a similar style.

by gas. Even in the wealthiest homes it was only downstairs that had gas lighting. Maybe it never occurred to people to install gas in bedrooms, perhaps worried about sleeping with it laid on close by. In 1878 the company issued a catalogue of appliances concerned with cooking and heating, prior to that it was lighting only. The lighting in the early days was from a naked flame, the mantle not yet having been invented and streets and the shops which remained open until nine in the evening were lit in this way. Until 1934 the lamplighter would regularly make his rounds but later on timers were fitted to the lamps. Today the street lights are electric although electricity did not reach Truro until 1927 when the supply was swtiched on by Mrs Lodge. The old photograph shows Fred Lance taking down Truro's last gas lamp, in The Leats. The modern view shows Steve Jewell of Southern Electric Contracting checking on an electric light in The Crescent.

Truro was one of the first places in the country to have a gasworks. As early as 1810 there was one on Lemon Quay, one of the first in the world. By 1822 there was some gas lighting in the streets of Truro and by 1877 there were gas mains all over the town, so all the streets and most of the houses were lit

The channel in the river is constantly being silted up and for many years Truro had a dredger in regular use. The *Tolverne* was the dredger from 1930 to the war years, when she was taken over by the Admiralty. She played her part in the war and went to the D-Day landing, then remained in London afterwards. Our river also had another part to play during the war. Prefabricated sections of Mulberry docks were unloaded at Tolverne and towed to Boscawen Park by London barges where the sections were then assembled. They were then launched and laid up on mud flats in the Fal until D-Day when they were taken to the Normandy beaches. Two

Chapter 3
THE RIVER

Mulberry dock tug commanders were stationed in Malpas. They were Lieutenants Kerber and Dupar.

ends in steps descending to the water. These days it is part of a pleasant walk-way alongside the river, which continues beyond the new bridge on to Furniss Island and, via the underpass, to Garras Wharf. The road leading to the bridge is lined with shops on both sides. In the past, Williams' fish and chip shop sold a really good helping of chips for 3d (three old pence) and Mrs Williams would give you a bag of scriddlings (knobbly bits of batter) for nothing. Other shops included Mr and Mrs Smith's grocery store and Hall's, the butchers. The entrance to Furniss's biscuit factory was in New Bridge Street and many school children paid a visit to watch the sweet-making.

The new bridge over the River Allen was constructed in 1775. Farther up-stream is the old bridge, which is a square rather than an arched construction and downstream is Boscawen Bridge, now part of Morlaix Avenue. In recent years some footbridges have been added. One leads from the shoppers' car park to the Riverside Walk outside the Royal British Legion and another is the private property of the flats on Ennis Quay. It is clear in the old photograph that the opeway leading from New Bridge Street

In this photograph, taken just after the war the area round Boscawen Bridge is a hive of activity. Local people have always enjoyed a trip on the river and two of the boats are *Skylarks* owned by Peter Newman at Tolverne. The other could possibly be the *Gondolier.* The bridge is the second Boscawen Bridge, built in 1862, the first one having been a rather unsatisfactory wooden structure. The building on the right has been at different times, Hicks' Garage, Penrose sail makers and Farm Industries. In the modern photograph the bridge which replaced the second bridge in the 1960s can be seen. It is much plainer in appearance and carries a busy main road, part of the Truro by-pass, known as Morlaix Avenue. The old

building has gone to be replaced by Haven House but just beyond that, to the left, the pointed roof of the Old Mansion House can be seen still standing after three hundred years.

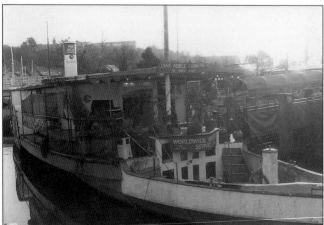

When the new gasworks at Newham came into operation in 1955 the old works, near Lemon Quay, were demolished. This had been the site of a gasworks since the early 1800s. It was one of the first in the country and some of Truro's streets were lit by gas in the 1820s. The works at Newham had a short life span as use of North Sea gas made gasworks obsolete. Today, standing on the bridge by Lemon Quay car park gives us a view of Jane Adelc's florist shop. This is situated on a boat moored in the river - the old paddle steamer *Compton Castle* which spent many years in Kingsbridge, Devon, before coming to Truro and starting its Cornish life as a restaurant.

One of the many quays in Truro where ships could be loaded or unloaded, was Town Quay, seen here around 1910. According to Kelly's Directory of 1914, the little shop on the quay was, not surprisingly, known as Town Quay Stores and was the premises of J. Edwards and Sons. They are listed as being 'Implement, manure, seed and forage merchants'. The name of the boat is not known but as usual, when a camera appeared, two little boys were happy to pose. There have been many changes in the riverside area, especially with the building of Morlaix Avenue. Both photographs show the tide out and it is particularly noticeable in the new one that Truro needed the services of a

dredger although the folly was that the dredger would dump all the silt down river and in time it all washed up to the town again.

The *JNR* of *Plymouth* was a stone barge used to carry stone from Calstock. Another famous stone barge was *Shamrock*, now preserved on the quayside at Cothele. The gravel, brought by sea, was used for road works and was delivered either to the Truro yard or to Tresillian. At one time Penroses were the agents for the stone. The *JNR* is seen moored up facing the lock gate in 1949. Today there is still trade by sea as Truro has a thriving port, but it is at Lighterage Quay where most of the work is carried out. The modern view is taken from Garras Wharf, which is now home to a large Tesco supermarket and car park, with a riverside walk. Almost the same view can be captured from this walkway. The *Skylark* is moored on the far side of Worth's Quay, which does not look quite so pretty without its pavilion.

The most noticeable change, looking across Worth's Quay to Phoenix Wharf, is the arrival of Radio Cornwall. Blewett's have had their bakery in Malpas Road for quite some time and the smell of freshly-made pasties wafts around, causing people who are not hungry at all, to suddenly really fancy a pasty! The building used by Tapper Motor Company has recently become the Treloggan Pine Warehouse and has an extensive selection of furniture inside. Radio Cornwall occupies the site where previously several warehouses stood and the car park for their staff and visitors is where the Admiral Boscawen pub was, prior to its demolition in 1966. Radio Cornwall has now been there for eighteen years and not only do they

broadcast from inside the building but it is not unusual in the summer for interviews to be carried out in the fresh air on Worth's Quay.

its place. The older photograph was taken in the 1960s and we can see, above and to the left of the subway sign, the building which was opened in 1858 and called The Church of England Training College for Girls. It was at the top of Agar Road and used as a teacher training college until the 1930s. By the time it was demolished it had been the Ministry of Agriculture building for some time. St Paul's church is seen almost hidden by warehouse buildings. In the modern photograph the old college has gone and the large Devington Hall building dominates the skyline. The church is obscured by trees but a part of the old Truro smelting works is visible beside the mast of the boat and the Radio Cornwall building is on Phoenix Wharf.

Worth's Quay has changed over the years. In 1911 an attractive shelter was built, a nice place to wait for the boat to go on a river trip. The shelter has gone now and seats and shrubs take

An old sailing boat is moored by The Green, *c.* 1920. To the left of the boat a car park attendant's hut can be seen through the trees. The hut is in front of the customs house, known as Green House and the royal coat of arms can be seen over the door. In the new photograph a bridge spans the river but when the first view was taken the river was open as far up as Lemon Bridge. The old customs house has gone now and the building which at one time housed the Palace cinema and the Fighting Cocks Inn is currently covered in scaffolding. The premises of the Royal Bank of Scotland extend into Green Street, a part of their building in Quay Street having in recent years been Oscar Blackford the printers. Originally this part of the building was the town house of the Rosewarne family where Pitt the Younger was entertained and later Sewell Stokes, first clerk of the county council, entertained Tennyson.

have been pulled down and there is new development at the waters edge. On the skyline, Truro School founded as Truro College in 1880, and partly hidden above the *Emma Louise*, has expanded over the years. The modern photograph taken from the quay behind the harbourmaster's office has not one single working boat in sight, just the masts of yachts.

When all the quays and wharfs were in regular use for trade, the river was a hive of activity and much of this trade was possible because of the dredger keeping the channel clear. This enabled the larger ships such as the *Emma Louise* of Barnstaple to come right up into town. The warehouses in the background face on to Malpas Road and have belonged to different companies over the years, for example, Western Counties Agriculture, Cornwall Farmers, Farm Industries and Trounsons. Some of the old buildings

The older photograph, taken around 1960, gives a good view of the new bridge after which New Bridge Street is named. Dating from 1775, it is only new in comparison with the next bridge up-river which is the old bridge of Old Bridge Street and is a medieval construction. All the buildings on the left have now gone. This includes the building on the far left which has at various times been Hicks' Garage and Farm Industries. Also on Ennis Quay were W.V. Whitford, picture framer and cabinetmaker, a car sales room and Browns the decorators. Although the bridge is still there it cannot be seen in the new photograph because of the trees. On the left are the new flats on Ennis Quay and on the right more flats

in Sunley Orford House. Furniss Island is now part of the Riverside Walk and has flowerbeds and seats like a mini park but many people remember when it was home to Mr Peters's chickens.

Taken in the 1960s this view of the river flowing under Boscawen Bridge was taken from a high vantage point. One of the coaches is carrying an advertisement for 'Enterprise Furnishing Stores'. This was a shop owned and run by Mrs Pearn and her son John. It was on the corner of Ferris Town and St George's Road and many people paid for furniture in weekly instalments. Beyond the bridge is a building faced with a series of arches. This was the Furniss biscuit factory. Although they produced many types of biscuit and also many flavoured boiled sweets and sticks of rock, it was always the gingerbread aroma or the peppermints that most noticeably wafted through the town. The modern photograph was taken from the roof of Penrose Outdoors and we see the new bridge carrying a dual carriageway in each direction. The river is obscured by a roof, too dangerous to stand on to take photos. The biscuit factory has gone and modern flats now stand on the site.

The changes that have occurred in the Garras Wharf and The Green area have been tremendous. The building of Morlaix Avenue swept away many riverside properties and just as people are accustomed to the way it is now, more building is going on at the end of Lemon Quay and on The Green which will change the character of the area again. In the early 1960s, before Morlaix Avenue was built, there is a boat moored close up into town and all the buildings behind it have gone to make way for Tesco and its car park. If it were not for the roof of part of the harbour master's office and Lander's

monument (a small dot on the skyline) it would be easy to think you were in the wrong town.

Truro has been a busy port for a long time and the dredger kept the channel clear for the big boats to come right up into town. The *Aud* was a Scandinavian ship carrying timber and it used to come up as far as where Tesco is today. She was sunk in the Second World War. There have been many changes and the modern view is looking towards Lighterage Hill in the area where the *Aud* is photographed before the war. The railed area on the left is part of the new flood defence scheme but has seats and is a pleasant area to sit and watch the work going on at Lighterage Quay. The Channel Food factory, where fish is smoked, is the white building on the right with waves painted on it.

The *Princess Victoria* was one of the passenger steamers which worked between Truro and Falmouth. She began her career around 1907 and plied happily up and down the river for many years with other steamers such as the *New Resolute* and *Queen of the Fal*. *Princess Victoria* was taken over by the Admiralty in 1941 and never returned to Truro. In this picture she has a reasonable number of passengers, perhaps they have not all boarded yet as she is moored at Worth's Quay. Many photographs of the steamers show them heavily laden with passengers, probably more than would be allowed today.

Chapter 4

GETTING ABOUT

The Penzance to London bus rumbles into Boscawen Street, c. 1910. Surely they are not all waiting to get on! It could be a long and draughty ride on the open top deck. The bus is a Lancashire registered Leyland with solid tyres so it would not be a very comfortable journey. The hut, seen in more recent years on The Green as the car park attendant's hut, is in Boscawen Street and was used as a rest area for taxi drivers. The Red Lion at that time had taken over the upper floors of the next-door building with Farrow's Bank below. Today a First Western National Mercedes 811D Midi-bus, with a Plaxton Beaver body is more or less in the same spot but this is the No. 96 bound for Trelander, a somewhat shorter and more comfortable journey than the London trip.

Down on The Green, which has changed dramatically, we find a Truronian coach in 1963. Mr Harold Brown used to take his daughter to school in Penryn using a mini-bus so that he could collect her friends and classmates on the way. The business expanded and starting from having one Truronian bus in a garage at Redannick in 1963 he built up the company which still exists today. In the photograph is Ann Mead, who worked in the Midland Bank and is standing beside the mini, Joan Hooper (later Mrs Vincent) and Jill Brown (Mrs Lawley). Mr Brown has sold the company and retired but Truronian goes from strength to strength. Today we see an easy-access bus with passengers boarding on Lemon

Quay but they also have mini-buses and executive coaches and are many peoples' choice for a coach holiday with door to door service.

During the course of this book we have seen many forms of transport in the city from bicycles to boats and horse buses to minis. The taxi has always been in demand and the line of horse-drawn cabs queuing through the centre of Boscawen Street is a feature of many old photos. After the change to motorised taxis and a change of venue for the taxi rank, it is not usual to see so many in one place. Today there is rank in Princes Square and also beside the war memorial. Harold Brown is leaning proudly on his Austin 18 around 1950. He later had many other vehicles, including some elegant black Mercedes, used mostly for weddings and funerals. Nick Bull was snapped with his A2B people-carrier style taxi, named City of Truro, outside the railway station waiting for customers.

Jack Parnell was the proud owner of a Vincent HRD 1000cc motorcycle during the 1940s. He needed transport but with a young family he could not afford a car so was delighted when the chance to buy the Vincent came along. During the war he had done some despatch-riding for the fire brigade so he had some experience with motorbikes. He had even been shot at by a German plane returning home from a raid and only escaped by diving off the bike and into a hedge. The Vincent would be a collector's item today but as it was prone to going wrong and was very complicated to work on, he sold it and bought a BSA 'Golden Flash' outfit. Today motorbikes are much more streamlined and Barry Carveth sits astride his pride and joy, a BMW 650. Not only has he equipped himself with comfortable riding gear but he also has the mandatory helmet, something that was not a legal requirement in Jack's day.

71

The coming of the railway was a haphazard affair. By 1877 there was a service to Penzance from Paddington and branch line to Falmouth. The Cornwall Railway Company owned the line from Plymouth to Truro and then onto Falmouth. The track was the broad Brunel gauge of seven feet. The West Cornwall Railway owned the line from Truro to Penzance and the track for this section was standard gauge, four feet, eight and a half inches between the rails. By 1889 it had all become Great Western Railway and by 1892 the lines were all standard gauge. During the 1960s, Truro was a busy station and in the photograph it is easy to see all the lines and the signal box. There is an engine in the shed, another on the line and on the right there seems to be some shunting taking place. Today the signal box has gone and the sheds are used by Cornwall Farmers Limited, where we see more cars and lorries than trains.

Although the railway station is more or less unchanged there are several little things that show we have a different way of life today. The lovely old gas lamp on the platform has been replaced by an electric one and the water hydrants have disappeared. Two down-trains in the station together would be unheard of today as the line on the left is now the up-line. On the far left can be seen yet another train, probably going up the line with two more trains visible beyond that. In those days the station was painted in the GWR colours of brown and cream. Today it has all been freshly painted in grey and blue and we only see two trains in the station together. The one on the left has just come from

Penzance and is going up the line and shortly after its arrival in the station the down-train, Paddington to Penzance, arrived.

catered for trains to London, the North and Bristol as well as coping with excursions and special trains. There was also the marshalling yard with all the goods traffic. In 1960 we see some of the staff of the Truro depot. In the centre front is the station master, Les Pullman, with the station announcer behind him. On either side of her are refreshment room staff. In the back row, third from right is Ken Vigus, standing beside Ken Boyns. The picture also includes: John Kenward (booking office), Mr Harper (signalman), Bert Waite, Vernon Knight and Mr Dodd (shunter). Today the station has two full-time and two part-time staff. The gentleman in the booking office was too busy to be photographed but platform staff Patricia Miles had just overseen the departure of a train.

Industries that used to provide work for many people are now scaled down, computerized and mechanized, so that less staff are needed. Truro Railway Station before the Second World War was a very busy place. It

Over the years many musical groups have come and gone in Truro. The Cornish are naturally musical and many people have a talent that they put to good use, for their own and other peoples' enjoyment. The Truro Imperial Five Dance Band attended a garden fete at St Paul's church in 1935. From left to right: K. McLean (violin), Bill Polmear (percussion), C. Vercoe (piano), Stan Polmear (saxaphone/banjo), Arthur Heayn (trumpet/saxaphone). From their outfits one would not know whether they were part of a cricket team or a band but the instruments would be a giveaway. Looking back over sixty-six

Chapter 5
SOCIAL LIFE

years, it sounds like a very genteel and pleasant way to spend an afternoon, at a church garden fete listening to music.

The older photograph was taken in 1927 and the Hope Inn was already an old building having been there for a hundred years or more. The swimming gala advertised in the window was to take place on 12 August and the Palace Theatre advertised entertainment entitled 'The Darling of Paris'. The figure of Hope is visible behind the gas lamp. The pub was demolished in the 1960s. The George and Dragon was demolished in 1931 and was on the site later occupied by Mr and Mrs Webber with their hardware store and central heating fuel business. Mr Webber had an extensive storage shed behind his property, possibly on the site where the George and Dragon had stabling for twenty horses with a large room above. Today St Austell Street is wider and well used as part of the ring road and Mitchell Hill leads to the magistrates' court. The building on the left of the old picture is today Williams the chemist and can be seen clearly in the modern photograph.

The ever-popular game of darts has flourished in Truro over many years. Most public houses have their own teams and here we see the team from The Barley Sheaf around 1975. From left to right, back row: Tom Russell, John Colston, Ken Coad, Roger Whitbury, John Edwards, Paul Gosling, Jack Leckie, Bill Penfold. Middle row: John Allam, Dave Wills, Taff Davies, Alan Bulpin. Front row: Ken Medlin, Joy and Phil Grimwood. Little John Grimwood is sitting on the bar. The modern team play at the Royal British Legion Club. From left to right: John Marsh, Chris Scoble, Terry Webber, Sid Vernon, Mike Webber, Kevin Pascoe, Paul Chapman, Dave Hill, John Allam.

running coach trips for their customers. By 1994 it had ceased to be licensed premises and was demolished some years later. On the left of the photograph are the gateposts of Gas House, home of the foreman of the gasworks. This was an elegant double-fronted house with a pathway to the front door flanked by lawns and gardens. At one time it was home to Mr and Mrs Jackson, Marlene and Keith. Now the character of the road has changed completely with all the buildings on the left being demolished and building work in progress for the new development on Lemon Quay.

Many streets which these days are lined with business premises used to be home to many people who lived in the cottages on either side. Fairmantle Street was no exception and the turnout for the street party held to celebrate Victory Over Japan Day in 1946 shows what a community lived there. The only name given in this photograph is that of Mrs Emma Solomon, the white-haired lady seated back left. She and her husband Charlie were the landlords of the Navy Arms in Fairmantle Street for many years, from 1924-1959. The pub was probably the heart of the community, among other services

These are two Truro bands from 1924 and 2001. The 1924 Truro Town Band were the prize-winners at Crystal Palace that year. From back left: W.J. Roberts Snr., H. Heayn, J.S. Penrose, R. Hosking, W. Champion, E.J. Trewhela, L.C. Wills, A. Smale, E.J. Heayn, R.G. Roberts, M.G. Hankin. Front row: H. Burgess, F.C. Pentecost, W. Fillbrook, H.S. Rule, H. Champion, J. Cliff, W.J. Roberts Jnr., J. Robbins, Adolf Trewhela, F. Woolcock, C. Hawken, R.G. Farley, C.H. Sleeman; E. Tremain, H. Hocking, H.S. Broadhurst, T. Hubbard, Maj. A.W. Gill (behind the shield), J.C. Trewhela, W.G. Tremain, W. Dingle, C. Whitford, F.F. Trewhela, A.H. Heayn. The Truro City Band of 2001, shown prior to entering a competition at the Hall for Cornwall, where they were pleased to come third are: Stephen Gale, John Fillbrook, John Rickard, Sophie Pellowe,

Duncan Smith, Jeremy Smith, Felix Hall, Natasha Pellowe, Joan Smith, Donald Pellowe, Jeremy Harris, Shaun Pellowe, Ben Strange, James Bryder-Rowe, Robert Hallett, Stephen Smith and Dennis Smith. The Musical Director, Roger Polmear, is on the right of the picture.

Truro had many clubs and societies for the young. For the girls, as well as brownies and guides, there was a group of sea rangers, led by Miss Ena Coombe. They were to be found at Malpas on summer evenings. There

was also a group of land rangers. They are shown here, around 1963, in the TOCH room in Boscawen Street, where they had their headquarters. They include: Linda Hill, Yvonne Metz, Susan Hendra, Ros Wills, Mary Moses, Mrs Appleton, Janet Appleton, and Margaret Moses. There are no land or sea rangers in Truro now but there is still a strong guiding movement. Naomi Mitchell is serving coffee with guide leaders, including Maureen Vickers who is helping her. Naomi is one of the Tregothnan guides and is raising money to go to Switzerland to meet guides there and see something of their country. She has to raise the money herself and a coffee morning in the Municipal Buildings on a Saturday is a good way to start.

The Truro Girls' Friendly Society was chosen to go to the Empire Stadium, Wembley, on Saturday, 28 May 1937, to take part in 'The Highway to Health', a display by 5,000 girls of the National Council of Girls' Clubs. A team of 24 Cornish girls attended and trained vigorously for the event. When they were selected to take part they were delighted, especially as they were the only team that was up to the necessary standard in the whole of the West Country. The event could not be televised because the girls had bare legs. In the centre of the picture is Vera Gill, on the right is Enid Penhaligon and Edith Varker is peeping through from behind. A more up-to-date organization for girls is the Brownies; the 8th Truro

Methodist Brownies are posing with brown owl Maureen Pascoe, on the left and snowy owl Mandy Richards. They have just won the coveted Halford Trophy, a carved wooden owl (standing in front of Snowy Owl).

who were already in the Boys' Brigade Company founded in 1883, became scouts as well. By 1908 they had changed their uniform in favour of that of the scouts. The first Truro scouts were associated with what was then called St Mary's Methodist church (later St Mary Clement and now Truro Methodist) in 1934. Their second annual concert was given in 1956 and the photograph shows the first Truro Wolf Cubs as well. On the 8 October 2000 they held their ninetieth Anniversary Service in the chapel at Truro School and are seen here in a group photograph. The celebrations had started with a barn dance at Tomperrow Camp Site and ended with a service which was visited by the Chief Commissioner for England as well as the county and district commissioners.

The First Truro scouts were formed in 1910 and by October of that year had four Patrols. Baden-Powell himself had come to Cornwall earlier in the year to encourage support for the scouting movement and some boys,

Victoria Gardens officially opened on 20 June 1898 in the sixtieth year of Queen Victoria's reign. By the time of this postcard in 1911 the gardens were already thirteen years old and had flourishing palm trees, however it looks much emptier than today. The fountain was moved from Boscawen Street in 1937 and put in the centre of the lily pond. In the modern photograph the palm trees have gone but all round the park there are many trees, which are homes to grey squirrels, and there are more flowers everywhere. Even the bandstand has a circle of flowers round it and at the time the modern picture was taken there were magnificent camellias in flower. In the

summer the bandstand is the focus of Sunday afternoon concerts and at the top of the gardens the fish ponds always attract attention.

The Admiral Boscawen at the top of Malpas Road is almost ready for demolition in this 1960s photograph. The sign has already been removed, perhaps to go on the public house in Richmond Hill, which took over the name at that time. That house was formerly the Exeter Inn. Today this area forms part of the car park for Radio Cornwall, who have their headquarters on Phoenix Wharf. Part of the Palace building and the Britannia Inn can be seen in the old picture, a view straight across Boscawen Bridge. As in many areas of town, the modern views are blocked because of trees. Truro seems to have many more trees and flowers than it used to - a credit to the City Council Parks Department.

The Chain Walk has always been a popular walk with the people of Truro and it is interesting to see on old postcards that it is advertised as 'Chain Walk, Kenwyn, near Truro'. The walk is about a mile out from the city centre so was once looked upon as being out in the country. It leads to the lovely old church at Kenwyn, dedicated to St Keyne and built in the fourteenth and fifteenth centuries on the site of an older building. Diocesan House is beside the church at Kenwyn and has part of the top of the spire of the old St Mary's parish church outside the gate, and the cross from its top in the garden. Although the Chain Walk itself is largely unaltered, a wooden fence in the centre of the new

photograph hides a housing development whereas in the 1950s the field on the right was used to graze cattle.

Prior to the new cricket ground opening in 1961, the cricket club played their matches in Treyew Road on what is today the car park for the football club. This team from 1931 pose in front of their pavilion wearing a fine assortment of blazers. From left to right, back row: P. Matthews (umpire), -?-, Phil Hogan, ? Bennett, F. Fox, Vic Barnes, ? Gibson, A. Richmond (scorer). Front row: G. Tonkin, Bert Buzza, A. Lugg, C. Elliott, Fletcher Hambly. The first XI team of 2000 are sitting outside the pavilion at Boscawen Park. They are, from left to right, back row: Nigel Thomas, Andy Hancock, Chris Phillips, Peter Bolland, Mark Thomas, Patrick Ellis, Ken (Tiger) Bray (scorer). Front row: Ben Price, Steve Pope, Tom Sharp (captain), Chris Penhaligon, Stephen Gay.

The ceremony of beating the river bounds is carried out every six years by the Mayor of Truro. Truro's boundary is at Messack Point, St Just-in-Roseland. In 1969 the mayor was Councillor J. Arnold Hodge and he is seen performing one of his duties recutting the letters T.B. on the boundary stone. The mayoress, Mrs Violet Hodge watches together with the town clerk and the mace bearers. Another ceremony performed on the same occasion is the 'arrest' of a citizen for a debt and in 1969 the harbour master, Mr Whitehouse, 'arrested' James William Donald Vage for a debt of nine hundred and ninety-nine pounds, nineteen shillings and elevenpence three farthings. On the other side of the river at Tarra Point, Murray Smith was 'arrested and bailed'. The current mayor

is Councillor Mrs Jennifer Hosken, who is seen hosting a coffee morning in the Municipal Building in aid of charity. She is flanked by two fund-raisers and also in the picture is the prospective Conservative candidate for Truro.

perhaps a similar hat in cold weather. Even childrens' fashions change and the bonnet that Edith is wearing would be more likely to be worn by a baby. A toddler would be wearing a hat, probably made of fleece and with tassels or pom-poms. Mrs Tamsin Andrew and her son Daniel are crossing Boscawen Street in roughly the same place sixty-nine years later. Mrs Andrew's jeans, boots and warm top are mirrored in Daniel's jeans, boots and fleece jacket. The emphasis these days seems to be on items that are comfortable and casual. There was two-way traffic in Boscawen Street in 1932 but these days it is one-way. Even so, Mrs Andrew had to pick her moment very carefully as the traffic was constant in spite of it being a Sunday afternoon.

Fashions come and go and it is said that everything comes round into fashion again but it is unlikely that our modern young mother would ever have been seen wearing the outfit that was in vogue in 1932. Mrs Gladys Hocking is crossing Boscawen Street with her daughter Edith, who was about two and a half years old. The thick tights and shoes would pass as modern today and

The rural idyll, or maybe not! A
thatched cottage in a country
village sounds wonderful but the
reality of this cottage somewhere in St
Clement around 1900 was probably
very different. The roof is sagging,
one of the bedroom windows seems to
be falling in and all modern
conveniences would definitely have
been lacking. Nevertheless it is a
wonderful old photograph and we can
only be grateful to the keen
photographer who took it all those
years ago. The variety of birdhouses
on the cottage wall look in better
condition than the building itself and
the cottage garden is not a riot of
hollyhocks but a few sturdy cabbages.

It is tempting to wonder whether this
cottage has fallen down or has been
lovingly restored and is now a
valuable, sought-after home.

moored safely in this tidal creek. In the old photograph not only is there a sail boat but also a working boat. The logs may be being loaded or unloaded, it is not clear and as the photograph was developed several years ago from an old glass plate, no information is available. The lady who owned the plate said that her grandfather was interested in photography when it was in its early stages so this is believed to be before 1900. Coal boats used to come into St Clement, perhaps the wood was used in conjunction with the coal for fuel. The gentleman in the centre is wearing a dog collar so was possibly the vicar of St Clement at the time. The wooden building behind him has gone now but was believed to have been a hut for the working boatmen.

The creek at St Clement is a very beautiful place and is much used today for recreation. The walk to Tresillian is popular and boats can be

The manor of Moresk was one of the most important manors in Cornwall and the church of St Clement was built to be its parish church. According to the booklet available in the church, it was believed to have been built around 1249, possibly on the site of an earlier chapel or even on the site of a coastal fort. Fortunately, although over the years the interior of the church has suffered some restoration, the outside is largely unchanged. The house on the left was The Ship Inn at one time, Thomas Andrew being the last landlord. In many places in Cornwall it is possible to walk straight out of church and into a pub but these days it is private housing. It still has its lovely thatched roof but now has the addition

of three thatched porches, decorated with straw birds. The cottage in front of the church was where Mr Godfrey, the water carrier lived and his charge was one shilling to fetch water for a week.

PEEPS ON THE FAL. MALPAS.

Fortunately there has been little change to this part of the river over the years. Taken about one hundred years apart, these photos show two familiar houses. The ferryman's cottage still faces Malpas from St Michael Penkivell and the larger building on the right, which can be seen quite clearly in the older picture, keeps it company. This building was once a public house known as The Ship Inn and when it closed in 1852 a pub of the same name was opened on the Malpas side of the river. The most famous 'ferryman' was Jenny Mopus, real name Jenny Davis, who rowed her boat *Happy-go-lucky* across the river in the late 1700s and early 1800s. She died, at the age of eighty-two, in 1832 but she lives on in a painting in the museum at Truro.

The Park Hotel was so named because it was built on land belonging to the Park Estate and is seen here around 1930. It is at the end of Trenhaile Terrace and commands beautiful views over the river. It had been a public house for almost one hundred years by the time this photograph was taken. Since 1962 it has been known as The Heron Inn and these days an important feature is the small car park because while a few people walk down to Malpas, most take their cars and there is very little room in the village. Malpas has had its share of excitement over the years. Queen Victoria and Prince Albert stopped on their yacht just outside Malpas in 1846 and in 1865 the Prince and Princess of Wales transferred to a barge there and were rowed up beyond Sunny Corner. The Malpas Regatta is a popular annual event where the Mayor of Malpas is elected and plays a prominent role in the proceedings.

The post office at Bissoe was believed to have been started ninety-five years ago by the Moyle family. The post office and stores is the hub of many a small village but these days there have been many closures of such amenities and often the local headlines threaten closure of some village store or post office. In Bissoe, however, the sub-post office and store is very much alive although Julie, the sub-postmistress said that I would have to get up early if I wanted to actually see the postman! He arrives early each day in his van and does not stop for long. The wheelwright's shop shown in the engraving of the early 1900s is now a private house.

The King Harry Steam Ferry Company Ltd was founded in 1888 and made the first crossing in 1889. It was twenty-four years before a new ferry, built in Falmouth, was brought into service. It was when the fourth ferry was in use that it was converted to diesel electric from steam and the present ferry, built in 1974, is one of only six chain ferries in the United Kingdom. During the war years it was almost completely taken over by American forces and General Eisenhower was a passenger. Some believe that the name *King Harry* was from Henry VIII who used the crossing on his honeymoon with Anne Boleyn, but it is more likely that it is named after Henry VI. The Arundels of Tolverne had dedicated a chapel to 'Our

Lady and King Henry', although they did not gain the advantages they had hoped for. As the older ferries have been seen so frequently, the one in use in the 1960s is shown here together with that of today.

In 1927 the Truro City Volunteer Fire Brigade took delivery of its first fire appliance to be motorized. Until that time horse-drawn vehicles were used. The brand new motorised version was given the name *The City of Truro*. It was remembered in Truro's centenary publication as a 'monster of red enamel and shining brass', a description which would do equally well for the 1950s Austin shown here. The Cornwall County Fire Brigade was founded in 1948 and had its motto emblazoned on the door of the appliance. The Mercedes vehicle, one of the appliances used today, also has the badge on the door but more than this, it bears the name, *City of Truro*.